MW00574959

INTRODUCTION

As I sit down to write this book in the heart of semi-rural England, I wonder just what the tropical and subtropical scorpions would think if they knew about it! Probably not too much, for scorpions are,

Scorpions are one of the world's most feared animals. Many are very dangerous. Take care when involved in any way with a scorpion.

PHOTO BY DR. HERBERT R. AXELROD.

on the whole, reclusive and do not readily communicate with man.

Scorpions! Those strange, enigmatic, prehistoric-looking creatures that seem to strike more fear into the hearts of man than all the spiders in the world combined.

Scorpions! Who in their right mind would even consider a scorpion as a pet animal?

Scorpions! Where do they come from, how have they evolved, and what is their purpose on Earth? Like all other creatures, nice and nasty, there must be a reason why these eight-legged, sting-wielding mini-beasts inhabit this planet of ours.

In most of the four corners of the world you will find scorpions—small ones, large ones, and in-between—but in a container in the corner of the

den? Really! Certainly a scorpion pet would be considered by the majority of people as a very strange thing indeed.

However, scorpions are without doubt fascinating, all are reclusive in one way or another, and all have interested man, the scientist, for many years. Recently, I receive more and more letters from people keen to keep or already keeping scorpions and wanting advice. Recently much has been written about scorpions, but from a pet-keeper's view there is very little, thus I was tempted into producing this book as a follow-up to the one I wrote about tarantulas.

So, who does keep scorpions? Well, I do for one, although not as many as tarantulas. Most zoos with insect houses will have a small colony of scorpions, usually

Pandinus imperator (the Imperial or Emperor Scorpion). The general public are becoming more aware that scorpions are being offered for sale as pets, but many are ill-informed about conditions under which these animals need to be kept in captivity. As the interest in them grows, the need for specialized knowledge of the species and their care in captivity will become more urgent.

Certainly scorpions are not the most attractive of animals.

Their "Jurassic Park" appearance can be rather off-putting, but many thousands of people are already caring for at least one scorpion. Plenty are kept for research, especially into venoms, but many are kept as pets. Thus the time is right, I feel, for a guiding hand, in the form of this book, to be held out to those keeping or wishing to keep a scorpion. We can at least give them a fighting chance of survival in captivity.

Keeping scorpions is a very specialized hobby. They can be found for sale in many of the more complete pet shops. Scorpions are not kept for their beauty!

PHOTO BY DR. HERBERT R. AXELROD.

The Imperial or Emperor Scorpion, *Pandinus imperator*.

PHOTO BY VINCE HULL-WILLIAMS.

We can, of course, only do our best to imitate their natural habitat, for, in many cases, this natural habitat is either unknown or very sketchy. Little has been written exclusively about these animals, although over the years several arachnologists have cast their eyes over scorpions, some actually putting pen to paper. It is mostly within the pages of arachnological tomes or the deep dungeonistic realms of scientific papers and journals that we find anything concrete about scorpions.

Although members of the many orders of arachnids (spiders, mites, ticks, solifugids, and whipscorpions also belong) all, including scorpions, have eight walking legs, they are very different. Although many can be kept in captivity in a similar way to tarantulas, many do need special care.

In the class Arachnida, the scorpions (Scorpionida) number some 1200 species, of which only about 50 species are considered dangerous to man. Deaths indeed have been recorded and, obviously, great care should be exercised when dealing with these creatures. In many areas, for example Morocco and Tunisia and Arizona, there are some very nasty little beasts about and, here again, great care should be taken, especially when walking outside at night. Scorpions are, for the most part, nocturnal in habits.

They normally only show aggression if severely provoked. Their usual response on being disturbed is to run, scurrying away into the safety of a hole. In other words, they do not court the company of man and probably actually resent his intrusion into their private world.

By definition, lethal or highly poisonous scorpions CANNOT and SHOULD NOT be kept as pets. In England and some other countries a license is required by any individual or organization keeping or wishing to keep dangerous scorpions. In the U.S. there are no such uniform laws, though cities and even states may have dangerous animal laws restricting or prohibiting the sale of dangerous scorpions. Hobbyists must be aware of local laws and also should be knowledgeable of the identification of "bad" species.

Dealers who market dangerous scorpions should know something of the abilities and experience of a hobbyist before handing over the animal. There often are cases where a dealer is misled by his supplier and has for sale scorpions that could be a potential danger, the dealer being ignorant of this fact. This can make life very difficult when endeavoring to discover the species of scorpion you are looking to buy.

To recap, you should know about the animal and its captive

Heterometrus spinifer, the Forest Scorpion from Malaysia.

Heterometrus longimanus, the Asian Forest Scorpion.

PHOTO BY VINCE HULL-WILLIAMS.

requirements in advance of its purchase. You should be informed of those species that are dangerous, although it is unlikely that highly dangerous scorpions would be offered for sale beside the kittens, hamsters, and goldfish—but stranger things have happened! Your future relationship with your scorpion could be a long one and should be a happy one for both parties.

SPECIES LIST

The following is a list of some of the more familiar as well as less common scorpions that appear in pet shops or dealer lists at least occasionally. The ranges are broadly stated, and the common names used are those I have seen used most often. Note especially that common names vary from country to country, author to author, and year to year. Scientific names also change on occasion, though I have tried to use the ones that appear most current in the standard references. The following list is not meant to be comprehensive, of course.

Androctonus australis, Fat-tailed Scorpion, Africa

Bothriurus bonariensis, Chocolate Scorpion, Chile

Buthus judiacus, Black Scorpion, Israel

Buthus occitanus, Mediterranean Yellow Scorpion, Southern France and Mediterranean shores

Buthus occitanus israelis, Common Yellow Scorpion, Israel and Middle East

Centruroides exilicauda (*sculpturatus*), Sculptured Bark Scorpion, Arizona and northwestern Mexico

Centruroides hasethi, Haseth's Bark Scorpion, Lesser Antilles

Centruroides hentzi, Hentz's Bark Scorpion, Florida

Centruroides vittatus, Three-striped Bark Scorpion, Southeastern U.S.

Cheloctonus jonesi, Burrowing Scorpion, Southern Africa

Diplocentrus hasethi, Haseth's Diplocentrus, Lesser Antilles

Euscorpius flavicaudus, European Scorpion, Europe

Hadogenes granulatus, Granulated Rock Scorpion, Zimbabwe

Hadogenes troglodytes, Granite Rock Scorpion, Zimbabwe

Hadrurus arizonensis, Giant Hairy Scorpion, Arizona

Heterometrus longimanus, Asian

Heterometrus longimanus, the Asian Forest Scorpion.

Hadogenes granulatus, the Granulated Rock Scorpion from Zimbabwe.

Forest Scorpion, Southern Asia
  Heterometrus spinifer, Forest Scorpion, Malaysia
  Isometrus maculatus, Spotted Scorpion, Tropical America
  Leiurus quinquestriatus, Israeli Gold Scorpion, Northern Africa and Middle East
  Pandinus imperator, Imperial or Emperor Scorpion, Western Africa
  Parabuthus mosambicensis, Yellow Thick-tailed Scorpion, Kalahari
  Parabuthus transvaalicus, Black Thick-tailed Scorpion, Africa
  Parabuthus truculentus, Burrowing Thick-tailed Scorpion, Southern Africa
  Scorpio maurus, Israel
  Tityus cambridgei, Cambridge's Tityus, Ecuador
  Uroplectes flavoviridus, Golden-green Striking Scorpion, Zimbabwe
  Vaejovis flavus, Yellow Vaejovis, Southwestern U.S.
  Vaejovis spinigerus, Stripe-tailed Vaejovis, Southwestern U.S.

Readers will appreciate that for the purposes of this book it would be impossible to list the entire scorpion population of the world. I have chosen those that appear from time to time on dealer's lists and also those that should not be kept as pets under any circumstances. Thus only some of the above species will be available for captive keeping. At the risk or becoming repetitive, some of those listed are DANGEROUS, and you should check the descriptions under "Individual Species" before contemplating a purchase.

A *Pandinus* scorpion from the Machakos district in Kenya, Africa.

PHOTO BY MARK SMITH.

BASIC KEEPING & HOUSING

Scorpions have proved, over the years, that they can survive in the most strange, alien, and forbidding environments. Ancestors of the present-day animals were among the first creatures to invade dry land some 400 million years ago. Although their ancestors were sea-dwellers (marine creatures) highly successful in their underwater worlds, the early scorpions quickly pushed inland to become the forerunners of our modern-day scorpions.

To prove the theory that scorpions have been around for millions of years, many fossilized remains have been found. Some of the more recent remains have shown that, amazingly, scorpions were (and probably still are) able to withstand fire, flood, and earthquake, and today they could probably survive a nuclear blast. Indeed, some scorpions thrive in the wild near nuclear-test sites in desert areas.

Scorpions frequently are described as desert-dwellers, and while this is true in some cases, there certainly are scorpions living in rain forests and also in the cooler Mediterranean areas; a few extend north into Canada. However, as a general rule scorpions are absent from area with long, cold winters, most of

Joshua Tree National Monument, California. The Mojave Desert is a transition zone and a suitable area for scorpions. Scorpions are not restricted to the tropics.

Southwest Cameroons, Africa. A typical waterfall close to which scorpions may be found.

PHOTO BY PAUL FREED.

the species being tropical or subtropical in distribution. The generalization that scorpions are gregarious (i.e., they can live together in social groups) is only true in some species. There are a number of species that are considered "loners," only coming together in the mating season. Many scorpions may be cannibalistic when confined together in small terraria.

In general, the natural habitat, for the purposes of captive husbandry, breaks down into three main categories:

A. RAIN FOREST: temperature 70-75 degrees Fahrenheit, humidity 70-80%.

B. DESERT: temperature 80-95 degrees Fahrenheit, humidity near 0%.

C. MEDITERRANEAN TEMPERATE: temperatures up to 70 degrees Fahrenheit, humidity 50-60%.

This shows the differences in climates where scorpions are to be found in the wild, and these are the ideal conditions we should try to imitate in captivity. The following details will help in the initial setting-up and future maintenance of your scorpion's terrarium.

RAIN FOREST
A deep substrate (say 3 to 4 inches) of slightly dampened vermiculite or peat or a combination of the two should be laid at the bottom of the container. This makes an excellent base for the animal to

walk about on. An artificial burrow should be provided by means of a piece of cork bark or half a plastic flowerpot placed in a corner of the container. Cover the artificial burrow with a clump of sphagnum moss. This enables the humidity to be maintained easily by spraying the moss every other day. The substrate should not be sprayed, since this serves only to make the ground cold and the terrarium dank and unsuitable for scorpions.

Lighting is not necessary, nor is it recommended for scorpions. However, heating of some description will certainly be needed, especially in the cold months of the year. It is not recommended that heat mats be placed under the scorpion's tank, since scorpions often will burrow down to cool off and would meet only yet more heat if heated from below. However, heat pads are useful if placed on end at the back or side of the tank and controlled by a good thermostat that, once set, will keep the optimum temperature required.

DESERT

A deep substrate of sand is best for desert-dwellers; this should be laid approximately 3 inches deep. The ideal sand for this purpose is the grit sold in pet stores for budgerigars and other small parrots. This sand is ideal mainly because it is pure and clean. Sand obtained from building suppliers is likely to contain impurities which could be harmful. Bird sand also often is sold loose so that relatively small

Southwest Namibia where the terrain and climate are ideal for many lizards, snakes and scorpions.

PHOTO BY PAUL FREED.

In the western Cameroons, civilization means habitat destruction. This puts a tremendous pressure on scorpions and other animals living in these areas.

PHOTO BY PAUL FREED.

quantities can be purchased. Several coarser grades of sand designed for reptile terraria also are suitable and easy to purchase in the shops.

A shelter for daylight hours is a must for the nocturnal desert-dwellers, and half a plastic flowerpot is ideal. This can be concealed by the liberal sprinkling of sand over the top, which also will give a more natural appearance to the terrarium.

Desert-dwelling scorpions often live under stones and small rocks, so the introduction of these will make the scorpion more comfortable. Lighting is, again, not necessary or desirable; heating can be provided in exactly the same way as for rainforest terraria. Being desert animals, humidity is not natural and therefore spraying is unnecessary.

MEDITERRANEAN TEMPERATE

Within reason, the substrate can be anything you like, even gravel. However, I do recommend vermiculite, peat, or a combination of the two as being the best type of ground cover. The depth needs to be around 3 to 4 inches; an artificial burrow can be provided by a piece of cork bark or a half plastic flowerpot. I recommend that you cover the burrow with sphagnum moss, which can be sprayed occasionally for humidity.

Unlike tarantulas, scorpions rarely wreck their tank setup. In the case of the Mediterranean species, plants can be used. I would recommend greenery plants rather than flowering plants, including small ferns, ivy, etc. These scorpions are used to areas where there is moderately dense vegetation, so the planting of the tank gives a more natural appearance and makes the scorpion feel more at home.

Lighting is again unnecessary and the optimum temperature of 65 to 70 degrees Fahrenheit is normally covered by room temperature and by central heating in cold months. Where no central heating is available, you could use a small table lamp with a red or green bulb; by training the light onto the tank and controlling it with a good quality rheostat you will easily obtain the temperature required.

TERRARIUM

The proper choice of container depends upon the space you have available and the number of scorpions you intend to keep. Some species can be kept in social groups, but others are loners and should be housed alone. I have noted the definite loners in the individual species descriptions.

A tank can be anything up to 3 feet long for the larger species (i.e., *Pandinus imperator*) and perhaps 12 X 8 inches for smaller species such as *Scorpio maurus*. Really tiny scorpions such as

There are huge pet trade shows held in many countries of the world. If you are interested in scorpions or almost any other living pet, visit these shows. The location of the pet shows can usually be obtained from your local pet shop.

The Emperor Scorpion, *Pandinus imperator*.

PHOTO BY ISABELLE FRANCAIS.

Bothriurus bonariensis will be happy in 8 X 6-inch containers.

Keepers of large collections tend toward plastic boxes, which are not especially attractive to the eye. Thus I recommend glass or plastic aquaria, which are widely available in many sizes. I do also use a small greenhouse propagator (a type of cold frame greenhouse) to house a pair of *Pandinus imperator* scorpions; this also is good for rainforest setups and is easy to service. (This is an idea that I stole from some friends, John and Christine in Norfolk, who also keep *Pandinus* in this type of container and who are experts in setting up ideal environments for their many exotic animals. Thanks, guys!)

In fact, there is no end to the kinds of containers you can utilize to keep scorpions, all of which are essentially ground-dwelling (though bark scorpions, *Centruroides*, do climb well), but I do not suggest you dig around the house for unwanted domestic equipment! Aquaria are so widely available these days and are relatively inexpensive, so you can start your scorpion off with a new container without taking out a bank loan!

In fact, most pet stores and tropical fish dealers will have all the equipment you need as a scorpion-keeper, including the heat mats and thermostats. Thermostats can be an enigma on their own if you are not sure what you are doing. By far the best and most accurate is the type that has a sensor dangling inside the tank and which, once set on the dial, will turn heat pads or red light bulbs on and off as the temperature varies. This type of thermostat is the most expensive, but it is a case of you get what you pay for. You should take advice from the store keeper, who will be only too pleased to help.

Peat and vermiculite are both widely available in garden centers, where you also can purchase sphagnum moss. Bird grit is available from pet stores, where it often can be purchased loose by the pound or the kilo.

Whichever setup you are establishing, a deep substrate should be made available since scorpions, as burrowing animals, love to dig.

You also should bear in mind that the tank you choose should be quite tall and have a VERY secure lid (weight or strap it down if necessary) because one important fact when dealing with scorpions is to note that they CAN and DO CLIMB, even up glass! They possess extremely strong tails and legs, and if they can reach an insecure lid they are quite capable of pushing this off either with tail or pedipalps. Once the lid is off, they can scurry rapidly up the glass, over the top, and out. An escaped scorpion is not a very pleasant prospect; they can run extremely fast, disappearing into dark corners, under loose skirting boards, etc. The best bet, therefore, is to make sure they cannot get out in the first place!

The pedipalp or pincer of *Centruroides gracilis.*

PHOTO BY VINCE HULL-WILLIAMS.

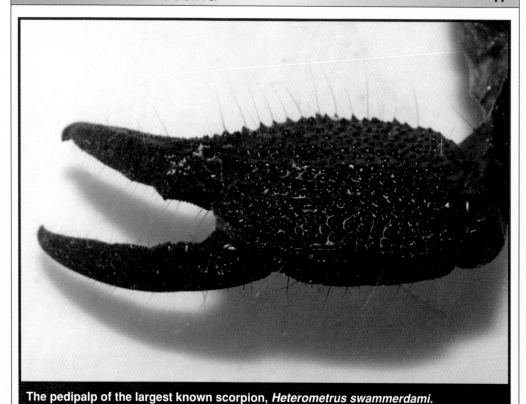

The pedipalp of the largest known scorpion, *Heterometrus swammerdami.*

FOOD AND DRINK

Drink

The large claw-like appendages that all scorpions possess are more generally known as the pedipalps or pincers. They have several functions, one of which is to help the scorpion to drink. The animal uses them as scoops, and therefore it is important to provide a suitable container for water in the scorpion tank. The dish you provide should be deep enough for the scorpion to scoop up water from it, but not so large as to allow small scorpions to drown. Here again, most pet stores sell suitably small dishes or you could use a plastic can lid if you are desperate. One common mistake is to fill the water dish with cotton wool or kitchen paper towel, which defeats the object and does not allow the scooping action described.

Food

Of course scorpions need to be fed! They are quite greedy in their eating habits. They can overfeed literally to the bursting point, so you should be careful to give only the amount of food the scorpion can immediately consume. For example, two large crickets at a time are sufficient for large scorpions. We feed our collection of scorpions and tarantulas on a weekly basis. Scorpions will take most large insects and, in captivity, the most usual food offered is crickets or grasshoppers.

In our case we use the common *brown cricket*, which is easy to obtain, easy to keep alive, and is bred commercially in tremendous numbers. Crickets and some grasshoppers (locusts) are easy to obtain, either through mail order or from local pet stores and reptile dealers. We keep a breeding colony of brown crickets to give us a reasonable variety of sizes to feed.

Food insects usually come in small plastic containers and need

PHOTO BY VINCE HULL-WILLIAMS.

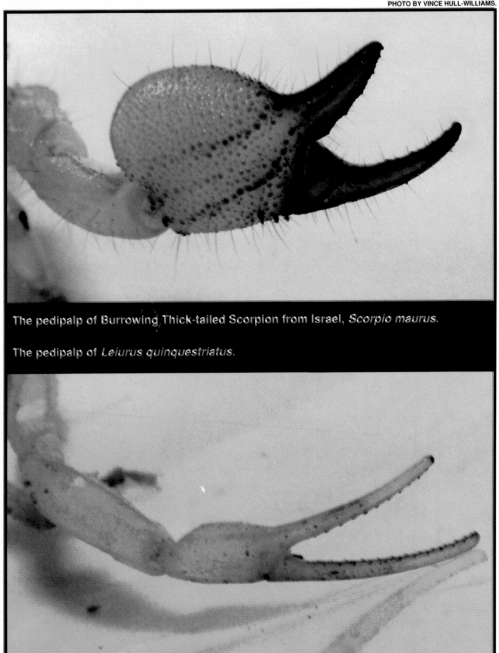

The pedipalp of Burrowing Thick-tailed Scorpion from Israel, *Scorpio maurus.*

The pedipalp of *Leiurus quinquestriatus.*

PHOTO BY VINCE HULL-WILLIAMS.

The African Locust, *Locusta migratoria*, is a suitable food for a pet scorpion.

PHOTO BY MICHAEL GILROY.

to be kept alive for at least several days, so a small plastic aquarium is ideal for keeping a colony of crickets. Instead of a substrate we use bran (from supermarkets and some reptile dealers) that is sprinkled liberally over the bottom of the tank. The less elaborate the tank furniture, the better for the crickets, which simply need hiding places. Thus cardboard egg cartons are ideal and can be changed regularly. Crickets thrive on a diet of the bran, fish food, and lettuce leaves. Additionally, commercially prepared cricket foods are available. An open container of water is dangerous to crickets (they jump in and drown), so only a very shallow lid of water with a piece of cotton or paper towel should be provided. The lid of the tank should be fine enough to keep in all sizes of crickets but

Crickets, grasshoppers and any bugs which move are all suitable for the diet of a hungry scorpion. This is the Black Cricket from western Texas.

PHOTO BY PAUL FREED.

A Short-horned Grasshopper, from Ecuador.

PHOTO BY PAUL FREED.

Any kind of cricket is suitable for scorpion food.

PHOTO BY MARC S. STANISZEWSKI.

The Malawi Grasshopper.

PHOTO BY MARK SMITH.

The familiar Green Grasshopper, *Melanoplus*.

PHOTO BY AARON NORMAN.

The Migratory Locust, *Locusta migratoria*.

PHOTO BY MARC S. STANISZEWSKI.

Newly hatched grasshoppers and crickets are more suitable for scorpions than some of the larger jumpers.

PHOTO BY MARC S. STANISZEWSKI.

cannot be so solid that moisture builds up in the terrarium. Crickets must be kept dry at all times or bacteria will build up very quickly. A wide strip of shiny plastic tape just below the edge of the container will help keep crickets from climbing to the lid and escaping.

Locusts (especially a type of large grasshopper from Africa) are certainly more difficult to keep and to breed, so only purchase locusts for immediate consumption. If you do wish to have a breeding colony, the basic container needs to be a tall specially made locust breeder that has a shelf above a plastic or metal tray on which two cups containing sand are located. The front of a locust breeder is covered with wire mesh through which air can pass easily and the locusts cannot escape. The container needs to contain some tall twigs upon which the locusts can climb to allow them to molt. The locust breeder needs to be kept at a temperature of 95 degrees Fahrenheit, using a white light bulb that is essential for keeping locusts alive. If the temperature drops below 90 degrees Fahrenheit, then the locusts will certainly die.

Feeding locusts is particularly important. They require a daily supply of dry grass, topped up with wheat bran and hay. The food provided should never be wet. Hygiene is vital, and their container needs to be cleaned daily by removing old grass, feces, and dead locusts. This routine is particularly important since locusts cannot survive in a germ-filled atmosphere. From this basic guide you will see why I suggest you buy only those locusts that you can use immediately!

The Giant Hairy Scorpion, *Hadrurus arizonensis* from the Mojave Desert.

WHICH SCORPION?

The species seen most often for sale to the general pet-buying public probably is *Pandinus imperator*, which is a very large and bulky scorpion with the common name of Imperial or Emperor Scorpion. In the U.S. you may well encounter *Hadrurus arizonensis* (formerly called *H. hirsutus*), which carries the common name of Giant Hairy Scorpion. You are unlikely to encounter the species considered the largest in the world (and probably just as well!), which is from the Indian sub-continent and has the scientific name of *Heterometrus swammerdami*. A specimen almost 9 inches long has been recorded and so far has not been beaten! (The more typical maximum length of this species, however, is only 6.5 inches.) *Pandinus imperator* has its origins in western Africa, with hobby specimens coming from the Ivory Coast, Senegal, Sierra Leone, and Ghana. *Hadrurus arizonensis* usually comes from Arizona.

Other species that you may well see offered for sale on dealers'

The Emperor Scorpion is probably the most popular species of scorpion as far as pets are concerned.

The Malayan Forest Scorpion, *Heterometrus*.

PHOTO BY KEN LUCAS.

lists are *Heterometrus longimanus* (the Asian Forest Scorpion) and *Heterometrus spinifer* (the Malaysian Forest Scorpion). Although these two are less likely to appear on a regular basis, they both are easy to keep and make good scorpions for a beginner.

Lately, I have heard that some dealers have been offering for sale the Israeli Gold (*Leiurus quinquestriatus*), which sent shivers down my spine since this scorpion is considered highly dangerous. However, on further investigation it was discovered that the scorpion actually being sold was *Scorpio maurus*, which is not considered dangerous to man.

It does go to show that when it comes to exotic animals, and scorpions and tarantulas in particular, the common name can be a vital clue to identity or it can totally confuse. You cannot blame the pet store for these problems since they are governed by what the supplier tells them. Unfortunately there is no legislation covering the naming of such animals.

When you go to choose your scorpion, you should always select a specimen that is known not to be harmful, always bearing in mind that all scorpions have venom (normally only used to paralyze prey or attack predators)

Hadrurus in a dramatic pose.

produced in glands that CANNOT and SHOULD NOT be removed.

When buying a scorpion, check carefully the sting, legs and pincers, and the two feelers underneath (pectines) that are

It is ALWAYS advisable to have the terrarium ready before you bring the scorpion home. Scorpions should never be an impulse buy. Before you rush headlong into a commitment to

Heterometrus spinifer, the Malaysian Forest Scorpion's stinger in the tail.

PHOTO BY VINCE HULL-WILLIAMS.

used to feel vibrations. Check for any injuries and be sure that the scorpion is active when gently touched with a pair of forceps. You should be aware of which scorpions can live together in groups and which are loners.

any animal, you should ask yourself why you want to have this particular pet. This question should be doubly considered when it comes to exotics and trebly considered when talking about owning a scorpion.

IDENTIFICATION AND RELATIVES

Scorpions are an order, Scorpionida or Scorpiones, of the arthropod class Arachnida. The traditional classification of scorpions recognized six families, the Buthidae, Chactidae, Scorpionidae, Diplocentridae, Bothriuridae, and Vaejovidae, though today many specialists recognize several other families. Before going into any more detail on classification, this is a good place to mention a few of the many types of animals related to the scorpions.

Arachnids have jointed legs (usually four pairs) and are closely related to the insects, millipedes, and centipedes on one hand and to the crustaceans (shrimp, crabs) on the other. Unlike any of these animals, however, they lack chewing mouthparts and generally suck in semiliquid food that often is digested outside the body. Closely related to the scorpions are the arachnid orders Palpigradi, the tiny whipscorpions; Pseudoscorpionida, the pseudoscorpions; Amblypygida, the tailless whipscorpions; Uropygida, the whipscorpions; Solifugida, the sun spiders or windscorpions; Opiliones, the harvestmen; and of course the Acarina, mites and ticks, and Araneae, the true spiders.

The young climb onto the mother's back.

PHOTO BY VINCE HULL-WILLIAMS.

Centipedes like this *Scolopendra* are distantly related to scorpions.

Briefly, the solifugids have several common names, including windscorpions, sun spiders, camel spiders, and hunting spiders. They cannot truly be described as a spider since they do not produce silk or spin webs. Neither can they be truly described as dangerous since they have no poison glands. They are, however, notoriously aggressive and exceedingly difficult to keep in captivity for any period of time. Their appearance, with a pair of gigantic claws appearing to arise from the top of the head, leads to several species being offered in the shops on occasion.

Whipscorpions are common in the tropics, but the one that usually is available fairly regularly on dealer lists is the Vinegaroon or Giant Whipscorpion (*Mastigoproctus giganteus*). This really is a super little creature coming from scrub and desert areas in the U.S. and tropical America. A 3-inch black animal with a long and very thin tail (the whip) at the base of the abdomen, this arachnid is in no way dangerous, although its prehistoric appearance can make for a scary picture. The large pedipalps are used mainly for catching prey. This creature's

Millipedes are distant cousins to the scorpion.

PHOTO BY WIL MARA.

main defensive mechanism is its ability to squirt acetic acid (vinegar), which it does only when angry or suddenly disturbed. The Vinegaroon is a quiet-natured, slow moving creature. They are often seen for sale along with their smaller cousins and are extremely easy to keep.

Alright, back to the real scorpions. Which is which and who is who?

Identifying scorpions is not as simple as you might think. Merely from size and color you may think you have one species when, in fact, you have something completely different. The illustrations and photographs may well give some clues but you really cannot generalize on the subject of identification.

As a VERY BASIC rule of thumb to identification and taking just two of the families listed as examples, you first look at the pedipalps (the two claw-like appendages in front of the walking legs). The family Buthidae has very slender pedipalps, while species of Scorpionidae have fat pedipalps. The opposite applies to the tail: Buthidae often have fat tails and Scorpionidae have slender tails.

The terminology used in studying scorpions is quite specialized, but the following terms should allow you to get a handle on how a scorpion is made and let you understand what authors are talking about when you read scorpion literature.

Aculeus: the stinging barb
Anterior: the front
Denticle: a small tooth
Dorsal: top or back
Lateral: side

Median: center

Mesosoma: body excluding head and tail

Metasoma: the tail excluding the sting

Ocular: eyes

Pectines: comb-like appendages under the body of a scorpion

Pedipalp: large claw

Posterior: the rear

Prosoma: the head

Shagreen: sharkskin effect

Sternite: underside of one of the body segments

Tergite: top of one of the segments

Ventral: underside

Vesicule: bulbous part of the sting.

You should study scorpions and learn as much about the specimen in your care as you possibly can. Identification is never going to be easy for the pet keeper, and you cannot go by size and color alone.

The sternum (breast plate) on the ventral surface of the animal is a good guide to family identification. Buthids, for instance, possess a triangular sternum. The shape of the spiracles (respiratory pores) on the ventral surface and the location of the trichobothria (large sensory hairs) also play important parts in knowing which scorpion is which.

Mastigoproctus giganteus.

PHOTO BY AARON NORMAN.

A solifugid Wind Spider.

PHOTO BY VINCE HULL-WILLIAMS.

A Whip Scorpion.

PHOTO BY REID TAYLOR.

The birth of the Emperor Scorpion. The mother is always helping her babies to climb on her back, either from the side or from the front.

PHOTO BY ROLF BECHTER.

The functions of the pedipalps are basically threefold. Firstly, they are used as drinking vessels when the scorpion scoops up water from its drinking bowl; secondly, they act as pincers for grabbing and tearing prey (scorpions rarely use the sting for killing prey); and thirdly, they are a courtship implement waved during the mating dance and used by males to hold the female.

The functions of the pectines, which are comb-like appendages on the ventral surface between the legs, are those of touch, being the scorpion's means of feeling its way. Scorpions have poor eyesight and rely heavily upon the sense of touch. Thus the pectines play a vital part in the scorpion's survival.

The body of a scorpion consists of two main parts, the prosoma and the mesosoma. The prosoma is an unsegmented carapace with a pair of median eyes in the center and a group of lateral eyes lie on each side. Each of the seven segments of the mesosoma has one to five dorsal crests. The first sternite is greatly reduced and bears the genital opening above the genital opercula. In females these are fused in the middle, while in males they are partly or completely separated. It is difficult without a microscope, but males can be recognized by the presence of two genital papillae under the genital opercula. The second ventral sternite has the small plate to which the pectines are attached. On the underside you will find a small slit that is the opening to the book lungs. The tail consists of five segments and the sting. The venom glands are located in the bulb at the base of the sting.

For the purposes of this book, we can assume that the most likely species we will come into contact with as pet keepers will be the Emperor Scorpion, Asian and Malaysian Forest Scorpions, Chilean Chocolate, *Scorpio maurus*, and the Giant Hairy Scorpion. All of these are reasonably easy to identify by just looking into the container. The Imperial or Emperor Scorpion, for example, is black like the Asian and Malaysian Forest Scorpions, but the Emperor has a very definite shagreen effect on the pedipalps while in the other two species the pedipalps are smooth and shiny.

It is when we progress beyond pet keeping into the dusty realms of research that we need to be very clear as to what we are keeping in captivity.

Scorpio maurus **from Israel.**

PHOTO BY VINCE HULL-WILLIAMS.

HANDLING

Picking up a scorpion with the bare hands is not recommended under any circumstances. It is foolhardy, and the risks to yourself and others, not to mention the scorpion itself, are enormous.

The Emperor Scorpion.

PHOTO BY ISABELLE FRANCAIS.

sliding out the card before removing the tub. It's easy and it works.

With larger species the same method can be employed, using a larger tub, but the best method I have found is by using a pair of forceps.

Basically, scorpions are wild animals unused to being touched or handled in any way. They are best left alone to be studied in their terrarium, where they pose no threat to anything or anyone save their food.

Of necessity there will be occasions when you have to move the scorpion from one tank to another or must collect an escapee that has been located lurking under the wardrobe! There are easy ways of retrieving the animal without having physical contact.

Smaller scorpion species, generally speaking, are more dangerous—more venomous—than larger species. Thus moving them from container to container could be quite hazardous. The simplest way is to place a plastic tub or drinking glass over the animal, slide a sheet of thin cardboard between the tub and the substrate, and lift the whole thing into its new container,

When you grip the top (basal) segment of the tail the scorpion is immobilized long enough to be safely transported into a new container. It goes without saying that the terrarium or a suitable carrying container should be close by before you pick up the scorpion since, even though gripped by the tail, it will recover its wits enough to endeavor to climb up the forceps!

If a large scorpion is an escapee and is on the floor, the animal will be in a position to avoid capture with the forceps. The vast expanse of the animal room floor is his playground, and there is no way he will be caught if he doesn't want to be caught. However, a large plastic funnel can be dropped over the animal. As you need to act quickly when you have an escapee, a funnel and a piece of card should always be part of your animal room furniture.

It is rarely necessary to clean out or change a scorpion's tank but should you find it needs to be done, a method that works is to place the tank containing the animal into a very deep plastic bowl or packing box. By doing this, should the scorpion slip from the forceps it can be cornered in the larger container and will not be marauding across the floor into hiding places; it can be quickly picked up again and rehoused. You will, of course, have a freshly setup terrarium ready before picking up the scorpion!

When opening a scorpion's tank for watering, feeding, cleaning, or whatever, make sure you know where the animal is before you lift off the lid. If you have an artificial burrow or some rocks in the tank, you (probably) can safely assume the scorpion, if not on view, is somewhere beneath these hiding places.

Whatever you do, you must be very careful when working around scorpions. Their unpredictably is one of their most interesting features. Always remember that ALL scorpions are venomous, just some more so than others, and all will sting if you provoke them and they cannot escape your attentions. Avoiding the sting is far better than being stung.

Thus I repeat: it is best NOT to attempt to pick up a scorpion with bare hands or to allow it to walk on your hand even within the confines of its tank. Accidents are always worth avoiding, and, as the old saying goes, "Once bitten (or stung), twice shy."

Handling the Emperor Scorpion is NOT to be recommended.

MATING AND YOUNG

Sexing scorpions is not easy, and it is almost impossible without the use of a microscope. Even experts have problems. However, assuming you are lucky enough to have a pair of, say *Pandinus imperator*, then they will probably have been living together for some time. Unlike tarantulas, where you have to introduce the male into the female's tank and stand by lest she decides to make a meal of him, scorpions are less of a strain on humans when it comes to courtship, mating, and producing young.

The Emperor Scorpion eating one of her own young!

PHOTO BY PAUL FREED.

There have been occasions, however, when a female scorpion has attacked a male and, although she is not interested in eating him, has stung him fatally. I have actually known a pair of scorpions to kill one another by stinging each other at the same time!

Scorpion mating can certainly be a violent and sometimes strange phenomenon. Scorpions do not copulate as such, which gives rise to the thought that they have not progressed very much since their ancestors left the sea. Most male sea animals discharge their sperm into the sea water, letting the current do the rest. Copulation is therefore unnecessary since fertilization is external. On land it is different, so males and females have to achieve some kind of coming together to enable fertilization and therefore the continuance of the species.

Modern-day scorpions have developed a spermatophore (sperm packet) that enables the sperm to be transferred to the female without the water element. Mating has been described as a dance and, in the initial stages, there certainly is movement from side to side and backwards and forwards, with the male using his pedipalps as a calming device to keep the female quiet and both animals doing a great deal of tail-wagging. The preliminaries over, however, the actual act of mating resembles a violent wrestling match, double tag-team style. The male deposits one to several rather thick hair-like spermatophores on a rock or piece of bark. Each spermatophore carries at its tip a gelatinous blob containing the sperm. While holding the female's

A Guatemalan buthid scorpion with her offspring.

pedipalps in his, the male literally pulls the female over the spermatophores. She opens the covering on a sperm pocket between her last legs and goes over the spermatophore, in the process inserting the cap into her body. The sperm then are available for fertilizing the eggs internally.

After mating, the scorpions go their own ways. With scorpions that are gregarious in habit, living in social groups, successful pairings are frequently achieved. With solitary animals, mating is far more aggressive and apparently rather random.

Scorpions give birth to live young that immediately climb onto the mother's back, where they remain for several days to weeks. Once you observe the young hitching a ride, you should prepare a new tank so that when they climb down you can remove the mother before she begins eating the babies. Baby scorpions (or scorplets) are quite safe while on their mother's back, but once on the ground they become prey. If the species is one that is living in a group, you will have to think about removing all of the adults ahead of the mass migration of young from mother, since aunts, uncles, and cousins also will find baby scorpions a delicious change of diet.

Once the young are loose in the tank, you can help them to find their own hiding places by dropping clumps of sphagnum moss at intervals throughout the tank. This applies, of course, to rainforest or Mediterranean species. With desert species, the young will scatter under stones or

The Emperor Scorpion, *Pandinus imperator*, decorated with her babies.

PHOTO BY KEN LUCAS.

small rocks or, in some cases, burrow into the sand.

A word of warning: when removing the adult scorpion(s), also take out the water dish, which obviously will be too deep for the scorplets. You need something very shallow so that the young cannot drown.

Feeding baby scorpions should not prove a problem as they will take pinhead crickets and wingless fruitflies. Depending on the number of young you are supporting, you should include roughly two or three food insects per scorplet per week. Like adults, they are very greedy and should be fed on a weekly basis.

Scorplets need to be two or three months old before

Centruroides vittatus, the Three-striped Bark Scorpion.

PHOTO BY A.G.SMITH

attempting to find them new homes. Interest in scorpions is such these days that there should be no problems with distribution through tarantula and scorpion societies worldwide.

Centruroides vittatus carrying her offspring.

PHOTO BY A.G.SMITH.

INDIVIDUAL SPECIES

In this section I have endeavored to briefly describe the scorpions listed earlier in this book. When you read these descriptions, I urge you to pay particular attention to whether or not the scorpion is considered dangerously venomous. Additionally, take note of whether they are considered loners or gregarious in habit.

ANDROCTONUS AUSTRALIS—FAT-TAILED SCORPION

This species is considered dangerous and should be housed alone. It has its origins in North Africa, where it inhabits hot, dry desert areas. The Fat-tailed Scorpion is very common and is found in sandy areas, on sand dunes, and the brown-red desert soils. Occasionally one is located in a burrow. Slower-moving than most scorpions, it is extremely aggressive and certainly NOT recommended as a pet. The Fat-tailed Scorpion is exceedingly venomous and has been known to kill humans. You would need a lot of courage or a good all-around knowledge of venoms before keeping this species. It is NOT recommended for amateurs and certainly not as a first scorpion.

A yellow-bodied scorpion, the pedipalps and posterior segments of the tail can be yellow or black. The scorpion can exceed 4 inches in length, and the tail is exceedingly thick and fat.

The Yellow Desert Scorpion, *Androctonus australis*, is also known as the African Fat-tailed Scorpion.

PHOTO BY PAUL FREED.

Buthus occitanus.

PHOTO BY DR. R. KONIG.

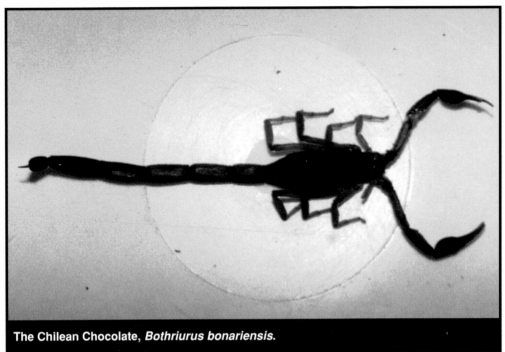

The Chilean Chocolate, *Bothriurus bonariensis*.

PHOTO BY VINCE HULL-WILLIAMS.

BOTHRIURUS BONARIENSIS—CHOCOLATE SCORPION

Species considered NOT dangerous; lives in social groups. This scorpion has its origins in Chile and often is offered for sale as the Chilean Chocolate. Its natural habitat is the Chilean rain forests, and this is the environment you should try to create for this species.

This tiny scorpion, no bigger than an inch or so in length, is a glorious shiny dark chocolate brown. Because of its size it will require a very small terrarium with somewhere to hide and a tiny water dish. Despite being so small (and the general rule that small is more venomous than large) this species is the exception that proves the rule and is not considered dangerous to man. I have found this scorpion easy to keep.

BUTHUS JUDIACUS—ISRAELI BLACK SCORPION

Species considered NOT dangerous, but it is a loner and needs to be housed alone.

This scorpion has its origins in Israel and is found in desert areas where it is hot and dry. Thus a

Buthus judiacus, the Israeli Black Scorpion.

PHOTO BY VINCE HULL-WILLIAMS.

Buthus occitanus, the Mediterranean Yellow Scorpion.

PHOTO BY VINCE HULL-WILLIAMS.

desert environment is the best habitat to create for this species in captivity. This buthid species is one of the exceptions to the rule which says that all buthids are considered dangerous. The sting, although painful, has no after-effects.

The Israeli Black is not very large, about 3 inches in length, and is black to greenish black on the body; the pedipalps and legs are brown, and the fingers are light brown.

BUTHUS OCCITANUS—MEDITERRANEAN YELLOW

Species considered DANGEROUS and must be housed alone.

Buthus occitanus has its origins in the South of France into Spain, where it lives in Mediterranean temperate conditions. The scorpion is light yellow to dark brown in color with dark bands on the tail. It is a small scorpion some 1 to 2 inches in length. This scorpion is very common in its natural habitat and has been known to be harmful to man.

BUTHUS OCCITANUS ISRAELIS—COMMON YELLOW

Species considered DANGEROUS and must be housed alone.

Buthus occitanus israelis is a desert-dwelling subspecies of *B.*

Buthus occitanus israelis, the Common Yellow Scorpion.
PHOTO BY KEN LUCAS.

occitanus. The Common Yellow is found in southern Israel and the Sinai and is light yellow in color and slightly larger than its European counterpart, being 2 to almost 3 inches in length. Like *B. occitanus*, it is very common in its natural habitat and is considered as dangerous to man.

CENTRUROIDES EXILICAUDA (FORMERLY SCULPTURATUS)—SCULPTURED BARK SCORPION

Species considered DANGEROUS and must be housed alone.

This scorpion has its origins in desert areas of Arizona and western Mexico and, therefore, requires a desert environment in captivity.

A medium-sized scorpion 2.5 to almost 3 inches in length, it is basically coffee-brown. It likes to live under stones and rocks and is considered extremely venomous. Its sting has been known to cause great suffering, and it has killed children. Though one of the most dangerous animals in the U.S. if no antivenin is available, it often is sold on dealer lists.

CENTRUROIDES HASETHI—HASETH'S BARK SCORPION

Species considered DANGEROUS and must be housed alone.

This scorpion originates in the Lesser Antilles. An island-dwelling animal, it makes its home in the rain forests of the islands off the Gulf of Venezuela.

Centruroides exilicauda from Sonora, Mexico.

PHOTO BY KEN LUCAS.

Centruroides exilicauda from Santa Catalina Island, Baja California.

PHOTO BY KEN LUCAS.

C. hasethi is about 2 inches long and is a coffee-brown color with the typical long, thin pedipalps of buthid scorpions.

CENTRUROIDES HENTZI—HENTZ'S BARK SCORPION

Species considered DANGEROUS and must be housed alone.

This is an American scorpion that is found in Florida. It is a buthid that likes moist habitats and lurks under bark.

C. hentzi can be up to 2.5 inches long and is a basically brown scorpion but sometimes with a distinctive cream line down its back and a spotted sharkskin effect on the legs and pedipalps.

CENTRUROIDES VITTATUS—THREE-STRIPED BARK SCORPION

Species considered MILDLY DANGEROUS and must be housed alone.

The Three-striped bark scorpion is a native of the southern U.S. from South Carolina to Texas or Arizona; it usually is found in dry, sandy pinelands. Though it has a potent sting that may be extremely painful, it seldom has any lasting effects.

This is a coffee-brown to reddish brown scorpion with three distinctive dark brown stripes running the length of its body. The basal segment of the tail is black, as are the main segments of the pedipalps. It grows to around 2.5 inches in length.

The Three-striped Bark Scorpion, *Centruroides vittatus*, with young on her back.

PHOTO BY PAUL FREED.

The Three-striped Bark Scorpion, *Centruroides vittatus*, with maturing young on her back.

PHOTO BY PAUL FREED.

CHELOCTONUS JONESI—
BURROWING SCORPION
Species considered DANGEROUS and must be housed alone.

As its name suggests, the Burrowing Scorpion is a deep burrower; it is found in South Africa. Although a rainforest

DIPLOCENTRUS HASETHI—HASETH'S DIPLOCENTRUS
Species considered DANGEROUS and must be housed alone.

This is another island-dweller from the Lesser Antilles, a rainforest species that burrows into moist earth usually under the roots of trees.

A pretty pseudoscorpion is the Peruvian Pseudoscorpion, *Cordylochernes scorpioides.*

PHOTO BY KEN LUCAS.

species, it prefers areas of dry, hard soil and thus dry peat probably is the best substrate for this species in captivity.

A small species an inch to under 2 inches in length, it is dark brown in color with black pincers and tail. The legs are slightly lighter brown and the sting reddish brown.

It is coffee-brown in color with distinctive cream lines down the sides of its body. It grows to some 2 inches in length.

EUSCORPIUS FLAVICAUDUS—
EUROPEAN SCORPION
Species is considered NOT dangerous and lives in social groups.

Euscorpius.

PHOTO BY DR. R. KONIG.

It is very common throughout southern France, where it lives in a Mediterranean temperate habitat, living in cracks in walls, etc. It is seldom seen during daylight hours. The European Scorpion also is found in small established colonies in the U.K. One is best known near the Ongar Railway Station in Essex, and there is another small colony near to the docks in Portsmouth. These colonies were established from scorpions that arrived in the U.K. on ships many years ago.

This is a small animal 2 inches long and is chocolate-brown in color.

HADOGENES GRANULATUS— GRANULATED ROCK SCORPION

Species considered NOT dangerous and lives in groups.

These are communal living scorpions natives to Zimbabwe, where they spend most of their life under rocks and occasionally under fallen bark. Thus a terrarium with both moist and dry areas is recommended for these scorpions, which must have large flat rocks under which to hide.

Considered to be non-aggressive, *Hadogenes granulatus* uses its sting very rarely.

This is a large species, 6 inches in length. The scorpion is dark brown in color and is well adapted

The Granulated Rock Scorpion, *Hadogenes granulatus*.

to life under a rock, being extremely flat-bodied and having the strange ability to lay its tail alongside the body rather than upright over the abdomen.

HADOGENES TROGLODYTES— GRANITE ROCK SCORPION

Species considered NOT dangerous and lives in groups.

Similar to *H. granulatus*, this is another flat and large scorpion spending its life under rocks. It comes from Zimbabwe and is considered one of the largest species in the world, growing to 7 inches in length.

Another dark brownish black scorpion, its entire life is spent

Hadogenes troglodytes, the Granite Rock Scorpion from Zimbabwe.

under stone slabs. It is considered non-aggressive.

HADRURUS ARIZONENSIS—GIANT HAIRY SCORPION

Species considered NOT dangerous, but must be housed alone.

This species used to be called *H. hirsutus*, but that name proved to apply to a different species. It lives in the deserts of Arizona, where it is very common. It can be aggressive but is not considered dangerous and indeed is a

Hadrurus arizonensis, the Giant Hairy Scorpion from Arizona.

recommended scorpion for a beginner. It requires a desert environment in captivity.

The animal is yellowish in color with long, obvious hairs on the legs. It can be up to 4.5 inches long.

HETEROMETRUS LONGIMANUS— ASIAN FOREST SCORPION

Species considered NOT dangerous and lives in social groups.

Another communal-living scorpion, this species is common throughout the Asian rain forests, where it burrows under tree roots and into leaf litter. The rainforest terrarium is ideal for this species, which enjoys warmth and humidity. I kept a male of this species for many years with great success and to the fascination of photographers for whom he would pose unashamedly within the confines of his tank. He became quite famous as the "dancing scorpion."

H. longimanus is black in artificial light and blue-black in natural light with smooth, fat pedipalps and a long, thin tail. The scorpion can reach up to 6.5 inches in length.

The venom from this scorpion is not considered dangerous to man, although a sting has been known to cause temporary (two hours) paralysis at the site of the sting.

HETEROMETRUS SPINIFER— MALAYSIAN FOREST SCORPION

Species considered NOT dangerous and lives in social groups.

This is another large scorpion that, like *H. longimanus*, can be over 6 inches in length. Another black or blue-black scorpion and not particularly aggressive in nature, this scorpion originates in the Malaysian rain forests, where it burrows into loamy soils near river banks and therefore requires a rainforest environment in captivity.

The venom is not considered dangerous to man, although, as for *H. longimanus*, a sting has been known to cause temporary paralysis at the site of the sting. The paralysis lasted only a couple of hours

The Asian Forest Scorpion, *Heterometrus longimanus*.

ISOMETRUS MACULATUS—SPOTTED SCORPION

Species considered DANGEROUS to man and should be housed alone.

This species is very common throughout the tropics in South and Central America, where it lives in mixed forest/desert environments. A combination of the two habitats will make the animal feel more comfortable in captivity.

I. maculatus is a basic coffee-brown in color with distinctive spots over the body and legs and the pedipalps. It grows up to almost 2 inches in length and is considered non-aggressive. However, the venom from a sting is considered VERY dangerous.

The Emperor Scorpion catching a grasshopper.

PHOTO BY VINCE HULL-WILLIAMS.

LEIURUS QUINQUESTRIATUS— ISRAELI GOLD SCORPION

Species considered DANGEROUS to man and should be housed alone.

This slender scorpion is around 2 to almost 3 inches long and is considered deadly! It is thought to be the most venomous and dangerous scorpion in the world. The Israeli Gold ranges from Turkey to North Africa and can pose very real problems. Its natural habitat is semidesert and, in Israel, it secretes itself under stones in the more hilly areas.

The body and legs are light yellow to orange-brown and the tail, especially in immature specimens, often is black.

Be very wary of *Leiurus quinquestriatus*—a pet scorpion it is NOT!

PANDINUS IMPERATOR—IMPERIAL OR EMPEROR SCORPION

Species considered NOT dangerous to man and lives in social groups.

Having dealt with the most evil, we now come to the least evil and certainly, in my experience, the least aggressive scorpion. This is the scorpion most often offered for sale (although lately importations have been somewhat restricted) and it is the species most used in advertising campaigns. Most zoo collections seem to have a colony of these scorpions in their insect houses.

P. imperator is a native of Africa, mainly West Africa, including the Ivory Coast, Senegal, Ghana, and Sierra Leone. It is a burrowing rainforest scorpion found mostly near river banks and occasionally under stones.

P. imperator can grow quite large, over 6 inches, and is greenish black in color with very rough pedipalps. The body is very bulky, the tail short and thin.

While the sting from this species would be painful, it is not considered dangerous to man and seldom can be provoked.

PARABUTHUS MOSAMBICENSIS— YELLOW THICK-TAILED SCORPION

Species considered DANGEROUS to man and should be housed alone.

Parabuthus mosambicensis.

PHOTO BY MARUS BURGER.

This burrowing desert-dwelling scorpion lives beneath rocks and logs in the Kalahari Desert and is common throughout desert areas in Botswana. It is a considerably well-favored delicacy for meerkats.

This scorpion is extremely aggressive and grows to around 6.5 inches in length. It is yellow in color. The venom from a sting is considered highly toxic.

PARABUTHUS TRANSVAALICUS— BLACK THICK-TAILED SCORPION

Species considered DANGEROUS to man and should be housed alone.

This is another desert burrower and can be found under rocks and logs in the wild. A basic black

Parabuthus transvaalicus.

PHOTO BY DR. R. KONIG.

scorpion that can grow up to 6.5 inches long. It is extremely aggressive and highly venomous, having the ability to squirt the venom up to a yard!

PARABUTHUS TRUCULENTUS— BURROWING THICK-TAILED SCORPION

Species considered DANGEROUS to man and should be housed alone.

This is a brownish yellow animal some 5 to over 6 inches in length. It burrows into loose, soft sand around the Ruwenzori River. This is another very aggressive and highly venomous scorpion.

Parabuthus capensis.

PHOTO BY DR. R. KONIG.

SCORPIO MAURUS

Species considered NOT dangerous but should be housed alone.

Scorpio maurus is the only scorpion in my species list that does not appear to have a common name. I suppose I could have invented one, but this would have given many scorpion experts and taxonomists palpitations to say the least, so I have kept my own counsel and *Scorpio maurus* is both scientific and common name for the purposes of this book.

This little scorpion is a desert-dweller living alone in sandy burrows. It is very common and is found throughout North Africa to Israel and the Sinai.

It is basically a yellow-brown to olive-brown animal around 5.5 inches long and is completely unaggressive. Fairly slow-moving as scorpions go, it is an ideal beginner's scorpion and can be found on dealer lists. Give it a small desert terrarium.

TITYUS CAMBRIDGEI—CAMBRIDGE'S TITYUS

Species considered DANGEROUS to man and lives alone.

This species from Ecuador has very little written about it, but it is a basic brown color and grows to a bit over 4 inches in length. It is found in banana plantations and therefore is considered a rainforest species.

UROPLECTES FLAVOVIRIDUS—GOLDEN-GREEN STRIKING SCORPION

Considered DANGEROUS to man and lives alone.

Tityus species.

PHOTO BY W. WUESTER.

This small scorpion comes from Zimbabwe, where it is found throughout the rain forests. The scorpion is dark green with golden markings on the legs and pedipalps. It grows to around 3 inches in length.

The venom is considered extremely nasty and, although not deadly to humans I would still class this as dangerous and extremely aggressive.

VAEJOVIS FLAVUS—YELLOW VAEJOVIS

Species considered NOT dangerous to man and lives in social groups.

The Yellow Vaejovis is found throughout the southwestern U.S., where its natural habitat is semidesert plains. Basically yellow in color, this scorpion is quite small, only reaching around 1.5 inches in length.

VAEJOVIS SPINIGERUS— STRIPE-TAILED VAEJOVIS

Species considered NOT dangerous and lives in social groups.

Another wide-ranging southwestern U.S.A. species, it is larger than *V. flavus*, reaching 2 to 2.5 inches in length, and is greenish yellow in color with a distinctive striped pattern down all segments of the tail.

Tityus species.

AVAILABILITY

Of course it can be assumed that few species from this list of scorpions will actually become available as "pet" scorpions, and some, indeed, it is to be hoped will never come into a pet store and be offered for sale. The notes below give my impressions of the possibility of each species being available in the pet trade.

Androctonus australis—unlikely to be seen in pet stores but has occurred on dealer lists in the past. Not recommended as a first or pet scorpion as it definitely is deadly.

Bothriurus bonariensis—occurs quite frequently on dealer lists and at fairs but unlikely to be in pet stores. Recommended as a first scorpion.

Buthus judiacus—I have never seen this one for sale, even on dealer lists, therefore unlikely to be in pet stores. Not recommended as a pet scorpion.

Buthus occitanus—unlikely to be seen in pet stores but has occurred on dealer lists in the past. Not recommended as a pet scorpion.

Buthus occitanus israelis—unlikely to be seen in pet stores but has occurred on dealer lists in the past. Not recommended as a pet scorpion.

Centruroides exilicauda—this very dangerous species occasionally appears on dealer lists but is unlikely to be seen in pet stores. Not recommended as a pet scorpion.

Centruroides hasethi—I have never seen this one for sale, even on dealer lists, therefore unlikely to be seen in pet stores. Not recommended as a pet scorpion.

Centruroides hentzi—this Florida species often appears on American dealer lists and occasionally is available in pet stores. Not recommended as a pet scorpion, though the sting is considered only moderately dangerous.

Centruroides vittatus—though common in nature, this species seldom is available commercially. The sting is not particularly dangerous, but it is quick and a great escape artist so it is not recommended as a pet scorpion.

Cheloctonus jonesi—I have never seen this one for sale, even on dealer lists, therefore unlikely to be seen in pet stores. Not recommended as a pet scorpion.

Diplocentrus hasethi—another species I have never seen for sale. Not recommended as a pet scorpion.

Euscorpius flavicaudus—often seen for sale at European insect/arachnid fairs, I also have seen this one in British pet stores. Easy to keep and makes a good first scorpion.

Hadogenes granulatus—this species recently has become available through dealer lists and even in a few pet stores. It is a fascinating creature to keep and study.

Hadogenes troglodytes—also recently made available for specialist scorpion dealers though still expensive.

Hadrurus arizonensis—I have rarely seen this for sale in the U.K., but the species is widely available in the U.S. and is considered as a very good first scorpion.

Heterometrus longimanus—this scorpion occurs now and again on dealer lists and often is seen at insect/arachnid fairs in Europe. It is an ideal first scorpion and is easy to keep.

Heterometrus spinifer—this scorpion occurs from time to time on dealer lists and sometimes is seen at insect/arachnid fairs. It is an ideal first scorpion and is easy to keep.

Isometrus maculatus—I saw this one offered for sale several years ago but it now seldom appears on dealer lists and is unlikely to appear in pet stores. Not recommended as a pet scorpion.

Leiurus quinquestriatus—occurs occasionally on dealer lists but always with the proviso of the scorpion being considered deadly. It is very unlikely to occur in pet stores and is a scorpion to avoid at all costs unless you are an expert.

Pandinus imperator—this scorpion is the one that occurs most frequently in pet stores, on dealer lists, and at insect and arachnid fairs. It is extremely easy to keep and makes an ideal first scorpion. Indeed, this is the species with which most people start their collection. It often gives birth in captivity. Massive

exportations in the last decade have led to efforts to control importation.

Parabuthus mosambicensis—I have never seen this one for sale on dealer lists and it is unlikely to appear in pet stores. Not recommended as a pet scorpion.

Parabuthus transvaalicus—I also have never seen this one for sale on dealer lists and it is unlikely to appear in pet stores. Not recommended as a pet scorpion.

Parabuthus truculentus—I have never seen this for sale on dealer lists and it is unlikely to appear in pet stores. Not recommended as a pet scorpion.

Scorpio maurus—this species has been available at insect and arachnid fairs and on dealer lists for several years. More recently it has been appearing in pet stores and is recommended as a first scorpion.

Tityus cambridgei—I have never seen this one for sale on dealer lists and it is unlikely to appear in pet stores. Not recommended as a pet scorpion.

Uroplectes flavoviridus—I have never seen this one for sale on dealer lists and it is unlikely to appear in pet stores. Not recommended as a pet scorpion.

Vaejovis flavus—I have not seen this one for sale in the U.K., but it occasionally is offered in the U.S. A fascinating small scorpion that would enhance any collection.

Vaejovis spinigerus—Once again I have not seen this one for sale in the U.K. but it is offered in the U.S. Another fascinating small scorpion.

STRANGE BUT TRUE

Scorpions have the ability to fluoresce! This strange phenomenon is known as biophosphorescence. The scorpion will glow blue-white under ultraviolet light, giving a ghost-like appearance. The use of a black light when searching for scorpions in the wild will produce this result and enable the searcher to find his quarry with ease at night when they are most active.

Scorpions glow under ultraviolet light.

PHOTO BY VINCE HULL-WILLIAMS.

Scorpions are rarely prey to other animals, although baboons seen to find them extremely tasty and, like the meerkats that also prey upon scorpions in the Kalahari Desert, they appear unaffected by the venom, consuming the entire scorpion. Meerkats usually bite off the sting before dining.

Scorpion venom often gives strange side-effects. A sting from *Heterometrus spinifer*, for example, caused slight paralysis at the site of the sting (a friend's index finger) and flu-like symptoms for an hour or so.

Way back in the 1950's, my father was stung by a scorpion that had arrived in the U.K. via a load of timber from Sierra Leone.

We can only speculate as to which species of scorpion was the villain of the piece, since it was quickly despatched to the great burrow in the sky courtesy of father's colleague's size 10 boot! The sting my father endured from the scorpion was extremely nasty. His hand swelled to three times its normal size, and the inflammation took four weeks to completely disappear. He had no other side-effects and no lasting problems ensued. I can confidently say, though, that if dad were alive today he would take a lot of persuading to come for a visit!

Scorpions remain somewhat of an enigma. Those that are available and that we can keep in captivity will teach us much and keep we arachnologists on our toes, learning more day by day. Love them or hate them, you cannot but admire their resilience, having been around in one form or another for millions of years. You cannot help wanting to know more about them, and I hope that in some way I have given you a new interest and a new aspect on arachnids.

EPILOGUE

So there you have it—the best guide I can give you to the keeping, breeding, and caring for scorpions. If you have any questions you would like answered please write to me c/o the BRITISH TARANTULA SOCIETY, 81 Phillimore Place, Radlett, Hertfordshire WD7 8NJ, England (a stamped addressed envelope or International Reply Coupon would be appreciated!) and I will be delighted to help if I can.

When you decide you would like to keep a scorpion, I urge you to think about it carefully. Remember, these are wild animals more at home in their natural habitat than in your den or animal room. They are unpredictable, sometimes aggressive, but always fascinating. Like most exotic creatures, they need and should

The head of a Sun Spider.

PHOTO BY WIL MARA.

have special care, and with this book I have set out to give as much information as possible in a language that is straightforward and, I hope, without too much technicality.

If you have trouble in acquiring specimens locally, there are dealers who have a mail-order service. In some countries (including the U.K. and U.S.) it is illegal to send scorpions through the postal system, but there are transport companies that provide this service and the reputable dealers will always use these companies. It is always worth sending off for dealer lists so that you can assess just what is available. You can thus decide upon the best setup for the animal you intend obtaining and prepare for its arrival in advance.

Good luck with it!